Anthony Gordon Pilla

Illustrated by
Courtney Christopher Amerson

PROISLE PUBLISHING

© COPYRIGHT 2024 BY ANTHONY GORDON PILLA

ISBN:
978-1-963735-80-2 (Paperback)
978-1-963735-81-9 (Hardcover)

All rights reserved. No part of this book may be reproduced or transmitted in any form or by any means, electronic or mechanical, including photocopying, recording, or by any information storage and retrieval system, without permission in writing from the copyright owner.

The views expressed in this work are solely those of the author and do not necessarily reflect the views of the publisher, and the publisher disclaims any responsibility for them.

To order additional copies of this book, contact:

Proisle Publishing Services LLC
39-67 58th Street, 1st floor
Woodside, NY 11377, USA
Phone: (+1 646-480-0129)
info@proislepublishing.com

Acknowledgement

A very special thank you to Lauretta Brooks, my wonderful life-long professional friend, who listened critically to the reading of my draft text, and helped me by checking errors in spelling, grammar, punctuation and word choice. Ms. Brooks made many changes to improve the readability of my work.

I wish to extend a special appreciation to Mohamed Murji for his support in compiling this project.

INTRODUCTION

In his 2004 State of the Union address, President George W. Bush called upon Congress to grant guest-work permits to nearly eight million illegal, mostly Latino, immigrants.

President Bush justified this policy by declaring that these immigrants would fill jobs American workers do not want! What impact would his proposal have on America's future? This Front Page format story will peer into the future to see what could happen!

TUCSON DIAMONDBACK

Weather: Hot & Sunny   Tucson, Arizona   August 14, 2001   35¢

REAGAN TO BUSH W. 43rd

WAVES OF MEXICANS CROSSING OUR BORDERS AS ILLEGAL ALIENS!

10-20 MILLION ARE IN THE U.S.A.!

2 | WAVE MEXICANA by Anthony Gordon Pilla

SAN ANTONIO ROSE

Weather: Hot   San Antonio, Texas   Thursday, Sept. 6, 2001   20¢

ILLEGAL ALIENS ARE "OVER-RUNNING" OUR BORDERS IN LARGE NUMBERS!

U.S. BORDER PATROL OFFICERS NEED HELP - NOW! • ARIZONA GOVERNOR CALLS FOR FEDERAL TROOPS!

WAVE MEXICANA by Anthony Gordon Pilla

SAN DIEGO SPIRIT

35¢   San Diego, California   Friday, October 16, 2001

American Embassy Reports:

50% OF MEXICANS WANT TO LEAVE MEXICO!
40% OF MEXICANS LIVE IN POVERTY
10% OF MEXICO'S POPULATION CURRENTLY LIVE IN THE UNITED STATES!

MEXICAN SMUGGLERS BRING IN UNDESIRABLE ILLEGAL ALIENS!

CITIZENS DEMAND: SEAL OUR BORDERS WITH WALLS AND FENCES TO KEEP OUT ILLEGAL ALIENS!

WITNESSES STATE: RV'S ARE FULL OF ILLEGAL ALIENS — MANY DIE FROM DESERT HEAT!

MORE U.S. BORDER PATROL OFFICERS ARE **NEEDED** TO SECURE OUR BORDERS!

LAREDO LONGHORNS
EXTRA EDITION

Vol 21, No. 163　　　Laredo, Texas　　　Friday, October 16, 2001　　20¢

MEXICAN INVASION!

TIDAL WAVE OF ILLEGAL ALIENS CROSSING OUR BORDER!

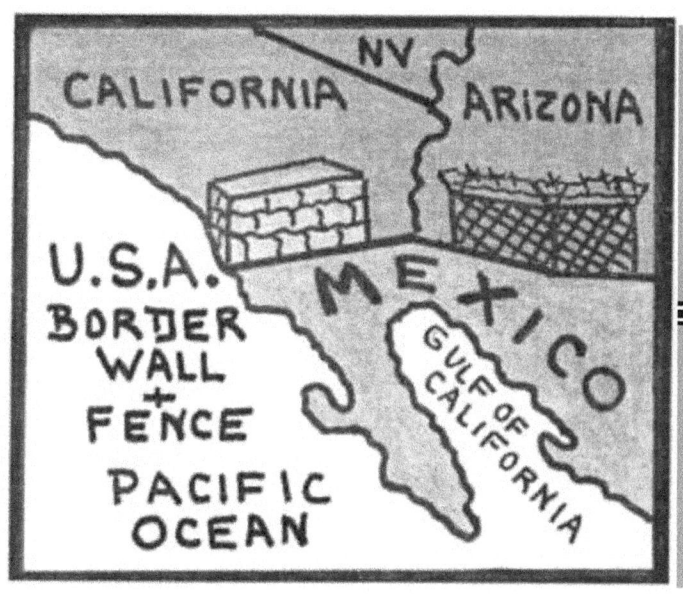

Mexican Smugglers Bring In **4,000 I.A. Each Day!**

Americans Demand: **SEAL OUR BORDERS!**

ARIZONA'S GOVERNOR JANET NAPOLITANO:

"Our Borders With Mexico Are Broken And Need Fixing By Washington!"

WAVE MEXICANA by Anthony Gordon Pilla | 5

SANTA CRUZ OTTER

20¢   *Santa Cruz, California*   *Monday, August 9, 2004*

ANCHOR BABIES DEBATE:

UN-AMERICAN TO DENY CITIZENSHIP TO ILLEGAL ALIENS; BABIES BORN IN THE UNITED STATES OF AMERICA!

3,000 ANCHOR BABIES OF ILLEGAL IMMIGRANTS ARE BORN IN THE UNITED STATES **EVERY YEAR!**

UPON REACHING THE AGE OF 21, ANCHOR BABIES CAN PETITION U.S. GOVERNMENT FOR PARENTAL CITIZENSHIP!

6 | WAVE MEXICANA by Anthony Gordon Pilla

Vol. 33, No. 129 Santa Fe, New Mexico Thursday, Oct 31, 2004 20¢

INTELLIGENCE BILL APPROVED BY CONGRESS!

Hailed by 9/11 Families

Bill Calls For 2,000 More US. Border Patrol Officers. President Bush Hired Only 210 New US. Border Patrol Officers!

State Department Renews "Travel Alert" For U.S. Citizens Going To Towns In Northern Mexico!

New Mexico's State Department of Education Recruiting Mexican Teachers For Three Year Teaching Contracts!

Movement in Arizona to Make English the Official Language of the State!

Census Bureau: 50% Of Illegal Aliens Are Uneducated!

Nuevo Laredo, Mexico: Chief of Police Executed!

WAVE MEXICANA by Anthony Gordon Pilla | 7

Final DEL RIO SPURS

Weather: Rain & Cool | Del Rio, Texas | Friday, October 29, 2004 | 20¢

"GUEST WORKERS"-Bush

10 MILLION UN-DOCUMENTED ALIENS NEED "TEMPORARY" LEGAL 3-YEAR WORK PERMITS!

THEY ARE WILLING WORKERS AND WE SHOULD REWARD THEM AS FARMERS AND DOMESTICS. HOWEVER, NO BLANKET AMNESTY!

OPPONENTS TO THE PRESIDENT FIRED BACK:

| Agricultural Jobs for Illegal Aliens is a "Sell Out" to the Farm Lobby + Corporations! | Build Walls or Close Our Borders Mean Little When American Employers Hire Them! | Farm Lobby: "Shut-An-Eye" to I.A. — WE NEED CHEAP LABOR ON OUR FARM! |

8 | WAVE MEXICANA by Anthony Gordon Pilla

Vol. 33, No. 165   Santa Fe, New Mexico   Thursday, Nov. 25, 2004   20¢

ILLEGAL ALIENS CREATING A CRISIS IN OUR NATION'S PUBLIC SCHOOLS!

HIGH DROP-OUT RATE IN CALIFORNIA SCHOOLS. 71% OF URBAN HIGH SCHOOL STUDENTS QUIT. STUDENTS HAVE NO CREDENTIALS FOR JOB MARKET!

Arizona's No Bilingual Classes Proposition Approved by Voters!

Danbury's Mayor Wants Connecticut's State Police To Enforce Immigration Laws!

As Many As 12-14 People Are Living in Crowded Homes.

High School Enrollment Went From 1,000 to 2,500 in 2 Years!

48 Languages Spoken in High School.

Washington "Wake Up" To This Illegal Aliens Invasion

- Critics Demand

WAVE MEXICANA by Anthony Gordon Pilla | 9

PECOS TUMBLEWEED
NITE EDITION

Weather: Rain & Cold | Pecos, Texas | Wednesday, January 5, 2005

I.A AND THE ECONOMY
CRITICS OPPOSED TO ILLEGAL ALIENS:

Economy Does Not Benefit Only American Employers Do!5

2.5 Million Jobs Created in 2004, But 1.5 Went To Illegal Aliens!

Federal Government Must "Step-Up" and Assume Responsibilities and Make Commitments!

Interior Of America Needs To Make Employers Accountable For Hiring Only Legal Aliens!

WAVE MEXICANA by Anthony Gordon Pilla

TOMBSTONE EAGLE

25¢ | Tombstone, Arizona | Sunday, January 23, 2005

BITTER BORDER BATTLE:
8,000 I.A. - CROSSING INTO ARIZONA **EVERYDAY...**

MINUTEMEN PROJECT: Created by Citizen Volunteers

NEIGHBORHOOD WATCH GROUPS TO ASSIST BORDER PATROL OFFICERS BY WATCHING AND REPORTING BORDER VIOLATIONS!

WAVE MEXICANA by Anthony Gordon Pilla

SAN ANTONIO ROSE

Weather: Rain | San Antonio, Texas | Tuesday, February 24, 2005 | 20¢

CRISIS IN FEDERAL COURTS!

40% OF FEDERAL APPEALS COURT CASES ARE ILLEGAL ALIENS!

BOARD OF IMMIGRATION APPEALS LACK SUFFICIENT JUDGES AND STAFF!

9TH Federal Court of Appeals Has 18 Months Backlog of I.A. Cases - Delaying Civil Cases!

I.A. CRIMINAL DATA BANK NEEDED FOR NATIONAL SECURITY !

Criminal I.A. In Detention:

65% Increase Over 2004! Electronic Detectors for Low Level Criminals - A High Priority Need!

12 | WAVE MEXICANA by Anthony Gordon Pilla

SAN DIEGO SPIRIT

35¢   San Diego, California   Friday, March 16, 2005

CALIFORNIA LAW ENFORCEMENT TO CRACKDOWN ON ILLEGAL CRIMINAL ALIENS!

LOS ANGELES POLICE To Reverse "Look-the-other-way Policy and Arrest Illegal Alien Gang Members Who Break The Law!

CURRENTLY...
30,000 Illegal Aliens are CONVICTED AND RELEASED!

ILLEGAL ALIEN GANG MEMBERS: "Walk The Streets Of Urban America."

WAVE MEXICANA by Anthony Gordon Pilla

AMARILLO CACTUS CITY EDITION

| 15¢ | Amarillo, Texas | Monday, April 11, 2005 | Vol. 28, No. 144 |

ECONOMIC FORCES IN AMERICA CONTROL IMMIGRATION POLICY!

SECURED BORDER IS ONLY A "SHELL GAME" IN WASHINGTON D.C.

Corporations Are Exploiting Cheap Labor in America!

AMERICAN BANKS Lending Homeowners Loans to I. A.

Slap in the Face of Law Enforcement!
Business Firms Accepting Controversial Mexican Government I.D. "Casa Martula" Cards For Illegal Aliens… Upon Hiring!

RECIPE FOR DISASTER!

14 | WAVE MEXICANA by Anthony Gordon Pilla

Vol. 39, No. 14   Yuma, Arizona   Monday, April 18, 2005   25¢

BUSH AND FOX AGREE:

GRANT PATHWAY TO CITIZENSHIP BY AWARDING LEGAL RESIDENCE FOR 9 YEARS!

UN-DOCUMENTED ALIENS GRANTED WORK PERMITS COULD COLLECT* SOCIAL SECURITY:

1. WORK 18 MONTHS FOR PARTIAL
2. WORK 9 YEARS FOR FULL

*upon returning to Mexico!

Critics State: Since Mexicans Have To Work 24 Years To Collect Mexican Social Security It Is An "Enormous Incentive" To Become An Illegal Alien And Work In The United States!

WAVE MEXICANA by Anthony Gordon Pilla | 15

SANTA FE TRAIL

Vol. 34, No. 95   Santa Fe, New Mexico   Tuesday, April 26, 2005   20

WAVE MEXICANA CRISIS:

WIDE RANGE OF OPINIONS!

"Guest Workers Do Jobs Americans Refuse!"

"Adequate Numbers Of Aliens Should Be Allowed to Enter"

"America Is A Place For Opportunity!"

"For Safe Border Crossings – Mexican Officials Will Protect It's Citizens With Instruction Booklets On How To Enter The United States!"

Illegal Aliens Are "Entitled" To Only One Right

D-E-P-O-R-T-A-T-I-O-N

Vol. 39, No. 34   Yuma, Arizona   Monday, May 7, 2005   25¢

MINUTEMAN PROJECT
VIGILANTES vs. PATRIOTS

PRESIDENT GEORGE W. BUSH:
I Call These Citizens - Vigilantes! Guarding Our Borders Belongs To The U.S. Border Patrol Officers!

SENATOR JOHN McCAINE:
MMP Tells How Frustrated Americans, Concerned With Securing Our Borders With Mexico, <u>Really</u> Feel!

GOVERNOR ARNOLD SCHWARZENEGGER:
We MUST Secure Our Borders! I Do Praise The Minuteman Project For Volunteering

WAVE MEXICANA by Anthony Gordon Pilla

SAN DIEGO SPIRIT

35¢   San Diego, California   Sunday, May 8, 2005

TALE OF TWO CITIES:

LOS ANGELES:

First Latino to be Elected Mayor of L.A., Antonio Villarraigosa, opposes the role of Minuteman Project in California!

His Motto: "Leave Your guns Outside The City."

FRESNO:

Mayor Allen Autry Calls For Federal Government To Close Our Borders For Two Years!

He Called On The California Mayors Association To Support His Demand To President George W. Bush!

WAVE MEXICANA by Anthony Gordon Pilla

25¢   San Clemente, California   Monday, March 23, 2005

BILLBOARD WAR!

LATINO TALK RADIO STATIONS ARE SUPPORTING BILLBOARDS WHICH "ENCOURAGE" ILLEGAL IMMIGRATION FROM MEXICO!

BILLBOARDS ARE ADVERTISING LOS ANGELES AS PART OF MEXICO, "NOT" AMERICA!

CITIZENS ARE PROTESTING TO STATE GOVERNMENT.

GOVERNOR ARNOLD SCHWARZENEGGER CALLED ON RADIO STATIONS TO REMOVE THESE BILLBOARDS!

CITY OF ANGELES (MEXICAN NOT AMERICAN)

WAVE MEXICANA by Anthony Gordon Pilla

YUMA DESERT SUN

WEATHER HOT

Vol. 39, No. 41   Yuma, Arizona   Saturday, May 28, 2005   25¢

KYL - CORYN: PLAN OF ACTION!

U.S. SENATORS JON KYL (R-AZ) AND JOHN CORYN (R-TX) WILL ASK CONGRESS TO HIRE 10,000 NEW US. BORDER PATROL OFFICERS AND 1,000 BORDER INSPECTORS!

ENFORCEMENT OF IMMIGRATION LAWS:

*AT THE BORDER
*INTERIOR OF AMERICA
*AT THE WORKPLACE

THE HEART OF THEIR "PLAN OF ACTION"!

STICK AND CARROT APPROACH

20 | WAVE MEXICANA by Anthony Gordon Pilla

SAN DIEGO SPIRIT

35¢   San Diego, California   Tuesday, May 31, 2005

CONGRESS VOTES FOR REAL I.D. ACT OF '05:

President George W. Bush Agreed To Sign Act Into Public Law!

HIGHLIGHTS OF REAL I.D. ACT OF 2005:

DRIVER S LICENSES:

States would require proof of Citizenship or Legal Residency in order for Drivers' Licenses to be used for Federal I.D. purposes.

ASYLUM:

Immigration judges to have more latitude in deciding creditability of someone's claim of asylum.

TWO-TIER LICENSES SYSTEM:

Act allows states to give immigrants certificates instead of licenses. Certificates cannot be used for Federal I.D. such as boarding airline planes! Act also allows states to issue temporary licenses to foreign visitors.

SAN CLEMENTE CONDOR

25¢   San Clemente, California   Monday, June 6, 2005

OPERATION: MEXICO SECURE!

PRESIDENT VICENTE FOX ORDERED MEXICAN TROOPS TO STORM BORDER TOWNS AND BREAK UP POWERFUL DRUG GANGS THAT HAVE, WITH THE HELP OF LOCAL CORRUPT POLICE, TAKEN CONTROL!

US. BORDER PATROL OFFICERS, F.B.I. AGENTS, I.C.E. (IMMIGRATION AND CUSTOMS ENFORCEMENT) AGENTS ARE ALL WORKING WITH LOCAL AMERICAN POLICE DEPARTMENTS, IN AN ATTEMPT TO KEEP THIS DRUG TRAFFIC FROM SPREADING ACROSS THE BORDER!

IN MANY TOWNS IN NORTHERN MEXICO, DRUG GANGS HAVE KILLED, AND EVEN KIDNAPPED AMERICANS, WHO HAVE "TIES" TO THE SMUGGLING OF DRUGS INTO THE UNITED STATES.

22 | WAVE MEXICANA by Anthony Gordon Pilla

SAN JOSE GOLDRUSH

25¢   San Clemente, California   Monday, June 6, 2005

FRESNO MAYOR CALLS For Immigration Action!

Mayor Allen Autry has called on Washington to halt all I.A. - for two years!

He would like to see a summit consisting of:

Local, State, National and Mexican leaders to develop a "solid plan" to cope with this human disaster!

Health care. Education and Courts/Jails hit hard by the "out of control" entry of illegal aliens!

WAVE MEXICANA by Anthony Gordon Pilla

LAREDO LONGHORNS
EXTRA EDITION

Vol 23, No. 131 Laredo, Texas Tuesday, June 14, 2005 20¢

NUEVO LAREDO CRISIS!

MEXICAN FEDERAL TROOPS BATTLE WITH "CORRUPT" LOCAL POLICE! VAST AMOUNTS OF DRUGS, WITH HELP FROM N.L.P.D., ENTER THE UNITED STATES FROM THIS BORDER TOWN. I.C.E. AGENTS REPORT THAT 98% OF ILLEGAL DRUGS ENTER THE U.S.A. FROM OUR SOUTHERN BORDERS!

AMERICA HAS A BORDER IN SECURITY PROBLEM, ACCORDING TO OUR IMMIGRATION AND CUSTOMS ENFORCEMENT AGENCY.

FREQUENT VIOLATIONS OF OUR FEDERAL IMMIGRATION AND CUSTOMS LAWS IS A SERIOUS CRISIS!

WAVE MEXICANA by Anthony Gordon Pilla

SANTA CRUZ OTTER

20¢   *Santa Cruz, California*   *Wednesday, June 22, 2005*

ALIEN COUNT

CONCERNS IN CONGRESS!

CONGRESS TO CONSIDER AMENDING THE FEDERAL CONSTITUTION, SO AS TO DENY THE CENSUS BUREAU THE RIGHT TO COUNT ALIENS IN THE "ONE MAN – ONE VOTE"

FORMULA: WHICH IS USED IN THE APPORTIONMENT OF REPRESENTATIVES IN THE HOUSE. CURRENTLY, THE 14TH AMENDMENT STATES THAT ALL "PERSONS" SHALL BE COUNTED.

IF HOUSE-RESOLUTION-53 IS PASSED BY CONGRESS, STEPS WILL BE TAKEN TO INTRODUCE AN AMENDMENT STATING THAT "CITIZENS", NOT "PERSONS" SHALL BE COUNTED.

REP. CANDICE MILLER (R-Mich) IS SPONSORING H.R.-53. REP. MILLER ADMITS THIS IS AN "UPHILL" BATTLE! AMENDING PROCESS IS LONG AND DIFFICULT, REQUIRING 2/3 VOTE IN BOTH HOUSE AND SENATE, AS WELL AS 3/4 OF STATES FOR APPROVAL!

WAVE MEXICANA by Anthony Gordon Pilla

25¢ San Clemente, California Thursday, July 1, 2005

BORDER IN-SECURITY
CRISIS!

AMERICA'S BORDER SECURITY POLICY IS FAILING AND BECOMING A NATIONAL SECURITY THREAT!

TENS OF THOUSANDS OF LA. AND OTHER THAN MEXICANS (OTM) HAVE BEEN CAUGHT CROSSING OUR BORDERS - ONLY TO BE RELEASED!

Why This CATCH AND RELEASE Policy?

1. Too few Border Patrol officers. Congress voted to hire 2,000 more - President Bush hired only 210, so far!
     We need 10,000 more to protect our Canadian and Mexican borders!
2. Federal detention centers lack beds!

SAN CLEMENTE CONDOR Editorial:

To secure America from terrorists and I.A, we need our President and Congress to act - NOW!

26 | WAVE MEXICANA by Anthony Gordon Pilla

EXTRA

SAN ANGELO PINTO

Vol 99, No. 193   San Angelo, Texas   Thursday, July 1, 2005   20¢

CONGRESSIONAL DEBATE:

ILLEGAL ALIENS OR UN-DOCUMENTED IMMIGRANTS?
EITHER WAY! THIS IS GOING TO BE THE
"HOT ISSUE" THIS SUMMER!

WAVE MEXICANA by Anthony Gordon Pilla | **27**

EXTRA
SAN ANGELO PINTO

Vol 99, No. 203   San Angelo, Texas   Monday, July 11, 2005   20¢

JUSTICE DENIED...

MEXICO vs. THE UNITED STATES

Mexico and the U.S.A. signed, in 1978, an extradition treaty. Criminal suspects are to be returned to the nation they may have committed a capital crime! In 2002, Mexico amended the treaty: they refuse to return to the United States, any Mexican who faces execution or life without parole, if found guilty!

Critics of this decision cry… This is an INCENTIVE to kill - Protecting killers!

28 | WAVE MEXICANA by Anthony Gordon Pilla

LAREDO 🐂 LONGHORNS
EXTRA EDITION

Vol 23, No. 131   Laredo, Texas   Friday, July 14, 2005   20¢

LATINOS FEELING POLITICAL POWER

Has Hispanic Vote In Urban America Come Of Age?

Latinos: Fastest Growing segment within the American Electorate	7.6 Million Latinos cast ballots in the 2004 Presidential Election. 80% More than in 1992

With 41 million Latinos in America - Will Latino candidates capture City Halls in America's Urban Cities?

The recent election of Antonio Villarraigosa as mayor of Los Angeles says – maybe!

Cities like San Jose. CA, and Hartford, CT have Latino mayors

WAVE MEXICANA by Anthony Gordon Pilla

NUEVA YORK

ENGLISH EDITION　　　New York, N.Y.　　　Friday, July 29, 2005　　　30¢

UN-DOCUMENTED ALIENS "SWAY" LEGISLATIVE ACTION AND POLICY IN CONGRESS!

Rep. Candice Miller (R-MI) introduced House Resolution - 53, calling for an amendment to the U.S. Constitution, banning aliens in the Census Bureau's "one man - one vote count, as required every 10 years. The 14th amendment states that all "persons" shall be counted to determine the number of congressional House seats each state is entitled.

Rep. Miller wants to replace "persons" with "citizens". She compared her 10th C.D. having 98% citizens to that of California's 31st C.D. with only 59% citizens. The I.A. population surge has given states like: CA, TX, and FL more House seats at the expense of states like: PA, KY, UT and OK which have lost House seats!

NYC

30 | WAVE MEXICANA by Anthony Gordon Pilla

Vol. 34, No. 185　　　Santa Fe, New Mexico　　　Friday, August 12, 2005　　20¢

STATE OF EMERGENCY
TO FIGHT
MEXICAN INVASION

GOVERNOR BILL RICHARDSON ISSUED A DECLARATION OF EMERGENCY TO ALERT WASHINGTON TO TAKE BOLD ACTION TO HELP STOP THE HOARDS OF LA. COMING INTO NEW MEXICO! THIS INVASION IS DISRUPTING THE ECONOMIC SECURITY OF OUR CITIZENS!

WAVE MEXICANA by Anthony Gordon Pilla

YUMA DESERT SUN

WEATHER HOT

Vol. 39, No. 142   Yuma, Arizona   Monday, April 15, 2005   25¢

CAMPO BORDER CONFRONTATION!

CALIFORNIA MINUTEMEN, IN AN ATTEMPT TO ASSIST U.S. BORDER PATROL OFFICERS FROM ALLOWING DRUG AND HUMAN SMUGGLERS FROM ENTERING THE UNITED STATES, WERE ATTACKED BY AN AGGRESSIVE MOB!

THESE PRO-IMMIGRATION SUPPORTERS KEPT SHOUTING: THE SOUTHWEST BELONGS TO MEXICO - NO MORE CLOSED BORDER - ONLY OPEN BORDER!

CLASH AT CAMPO

Final DEL RIO SPURS

| Weather: Hot & Dry | Del Rio, Texas | Saturday, August 27, 2005 | 25¢ |

ILLEGAL ALIENS ARE CREATING A NATIONAL MEDICAL CRISIS!

CRITICAL CONDITIONS EXIST AT MEDICAL FACILITIES IN AMERICA.

> 84 HOSPITALS CLOSED IN CALIFORNIA

I.A. Are Bringing Into The United States Diseases Such As: Polio, Hepatitis And Tuberculosis At An Alarming Rate!

CONGRESS ENACTED THE E.M.A.T. ACT:

<u>EMERGENCY MEDICAL ALIENS TREATMENT ACT</u>, WHICH IS PLACING DIFFICULTIES ON MEDICAL STAFFS AND CENTERS!

WAVE MEXICANA by Anthony Gordon Pilla

EL PASO LONE STAR

Evening Edition   El Paso, Texas   Monday, September 5, 2005   20¢

DEPORTATION OF I.A. GANG MEMBERS!

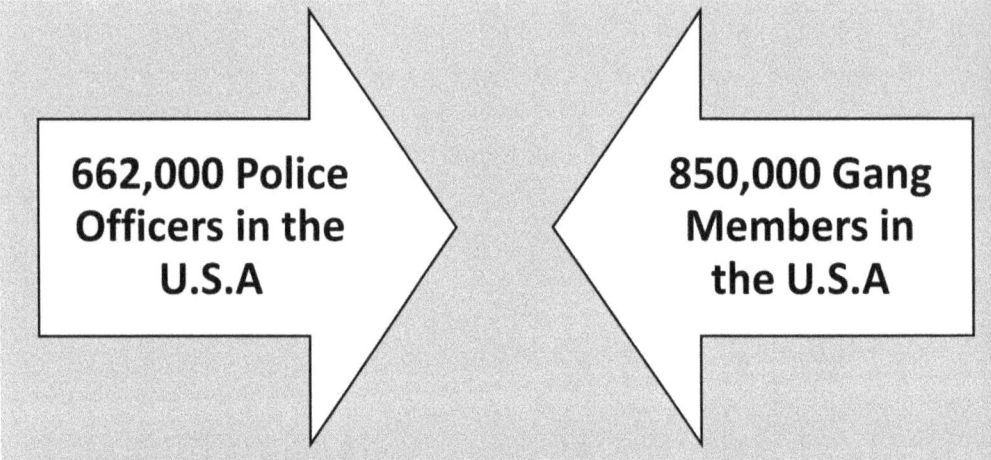

662,000 Police Officers in the U.S.A

850,000 Gang Members in the U.S.A

IT IS ESTIMATED THAT 60% OF THIS TOTAL IS COMPOSED OF ILLEGAL ALIENS, MAINLY FROM MEXICO AND EL SALVADOR.

It has been reported that it is difficult to deport captured criminal gang members! There appears to be a "loophole" in our immigration laws.

There is a clause: "Temporary Protective Status" which hinders deportation procedures. Congress is looking into this technicality.

75 Pesos   Mexico City, Mexico   Sunday, October 16, 2005

VERBAL BORDER WAR!

LATINO PRO-MEXICAN ADVOCATES DENOUNCE YANKEE-GRINGOS!

PECOS TUMBLEWEED
NITE EDITION

Weather: Rain Pecos, Texas Thursday, October 20, 2005 20¢

FEDERAL BORDER PROTECTION MILITIA?

Concerned about waves of Illegal Aliens crossing into Texas, Congressman John Culberson (R-TX) introduced House Resolution - 3622, which calls for a government sponsored CITIZENS PATROL CORPS to assist our border patrol officers in monitoring our borders with Mexico!

Rep. Culberson has 46 co-sponsors to his resolution.

Texas governor Perry was open to his idea, provided the militia was under sheriff's authority. Funding for this corps would come from unspent Homeland Security budget!

SANTA FE TRAIL

Vol. 34, No. 360   Santa Fe, New Mexico   Monday, December 26, 2005   20¢

ILLEGAL ALIENS HEALTH CARE CRISIS!

I. A. ARE CREATING SERIOUS MEDICAL PROBLEMS AT HOSPITALS ALL OVER THE SOUTHWEST!

84 HOSPITALS CLOSED IN CALIFORNIA DUE TO OVERLOAD OF I.A.

EMERGENCY ROOM CASES! MEDICAL STAFFS CANNOT KEEP UP WITH THE DEMANDS FOR EMERGENCY TREATMENTS!

CATCH-22:

HOSPITALS MUST VERIFY TREATMENTS ARE FOR ALIENS! MANY ALIENS REFUSE TO SUBMIT TO MEDICAL INQUIRY

FEAR OF DEPORTATION!

CONGRESS ENACTED THE *E.M.A.T. ACT* TO HELP PAY FOR *ALIENS'* MEDICAL COST.

CALIFORNIA RECEIVED $70 MILLION,

TEXAS - $46 MILLION

and ARIZONA GIVEN $45 MILLION!

WAVE MEXICANA by Anthony Gordon Pilla | 37

AMARILLO CACTUS CITY EDITION

| 15¢ | Amarillo, Texas | Monday, January 9, 2006 | Vol. 29, No. 9 |

BORDER WAR!

MEXICO

USA

BROWN BERETS vs. MINUTEMEN

38 | WAVE MEXICANA by Anthony Gordon Pilla

SAN JOSE GOLDRUSH

25¢ — San Jose, California — Friday, March 9, 2007

BATTLEGROUND:

ENGLISH - THE OFFICIAL LANGUAGE OF THE UNITED STATES?

YES

From the beginning of our Republic, all documents have been written in English!

Past immigrants tried to speak and write in English.

75% of Americans want Congress to declare English our language!

NO

To require let century immigrants to speak and write in English is not only racism, but also an insult to the various cultures of recent groups of immigrants!

We want America to be a **multi-lingual** nation!

LAREDO LONGHORNS
EXTRA EDITION

| Vol 28, No. 76 | Laredo, Texas | Friday, April 11, 2010 | 30¢ |

ETHNIC GROUPS:
SOUTHWESTERN STATES

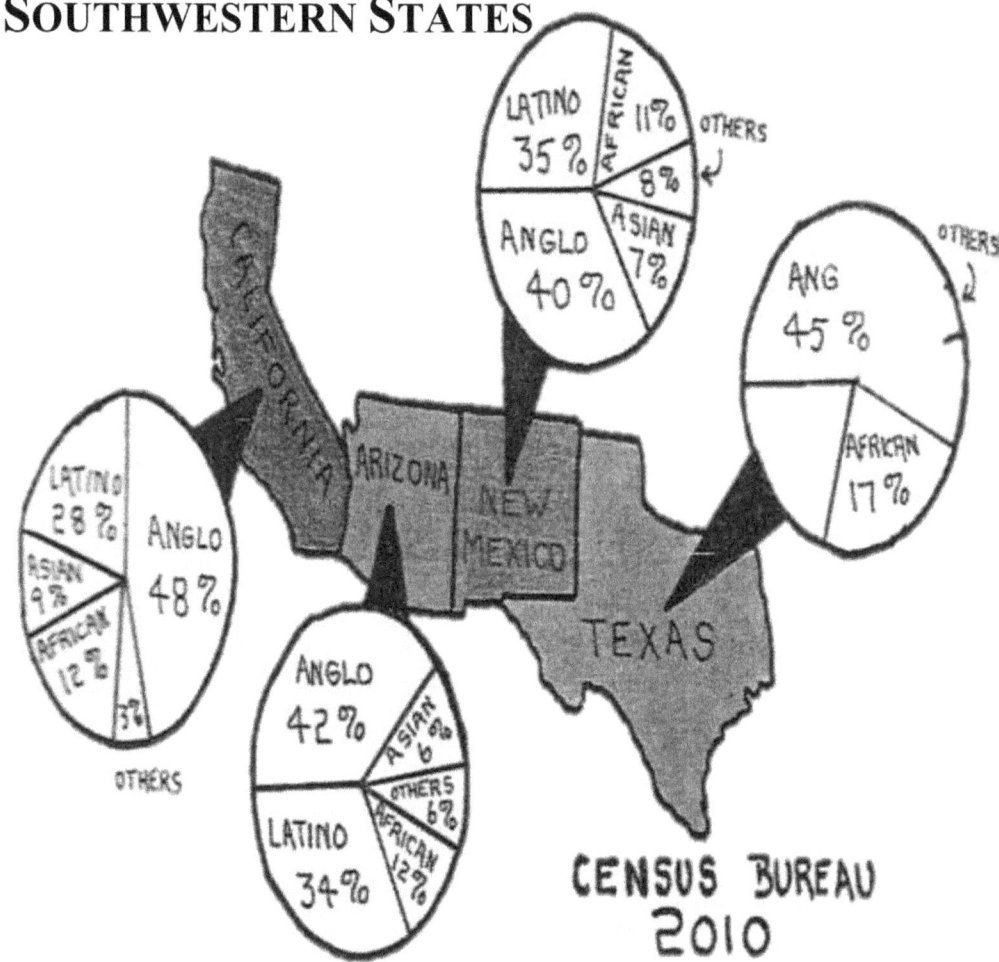

40 | WAVE MEXICANA by Anthony Gordon Pilla

PECOS TUMBLEWEED
NITE EDITION

Weather: Cold & Dry | Pecos, Texas | Wednesday, January 8, 2014 | 25¢

27th AMENDMENT FAILS
TO GET NECESSARY 38 STATES APPROVAL FOR RATIFICATION!
ONLY 35 STATES VOTED TO RATIFY...

BATTLE OF THE STATES
URBAN vs. RURAL

URBAN STATES
State legislatures with large Latino population voted against amendment. Amendment 14 requires the counting of all "persons" - Giving I.A. a voice!

Urban States: CA, NY, TX, FL, IL, OH, MI, PA, NJ.

RURAL STATES
State with high counts of Anglos have more citizens.

27th amendment calls for replacing the word "persons" for "citizen" - thus a lower state count - and a loss of house seats to larger populated states.

Rural States: ND, SD, KY, IA, WY, UT, KA, NH, VT, DL.

WAVE MEXICANA by Anthony Gordon Pilla

SANTA CRUZ OTTER

40¢   *Santa Cruz, California*   *Monday, January 1, 2020*

OTTER'S 2020 VISION FOR AMERICAN FUTURE!

1. 400,000 ANCHOR BABIES TURN 21 THIS DECADE, THUS CITIZENSHIP FOR I.A. PARENTS!
2. SURGE IN LATINO POLITICAL POWER IN SOUTHWEST!
3. SOARING COST TO TAXPAYERS: PUBLIC EDUCATION, MEDICAL FACILITIES, LAW ENFORCEMENT AND JUDICIAL SYSTEM!

Happy New Year 2030!

SAN DIEGO SPIRIT

50¢   San Diego, California   Monday, January 1, 2030

HIGHLIGHTS OF THE…

1) The "GREAT WALL" of California - Finally Completed!
2) It is estimated that America has, living in our borders, 35 million I.A. - a cost of $85 billion to support!
3) It is projected that in the year 2040, 50 million Illegal Immigrants will cost Uncle Sam $135 billion to provide them with vital social services!

PECOS TUMBLEWEED

NITE EDITION

Weather: Cold & Windy Pecos, Texas Monday, January 12, 2040 40¢

LATINO
LARGEST ETHNIC GROUP IN THE SOUTHWEST!

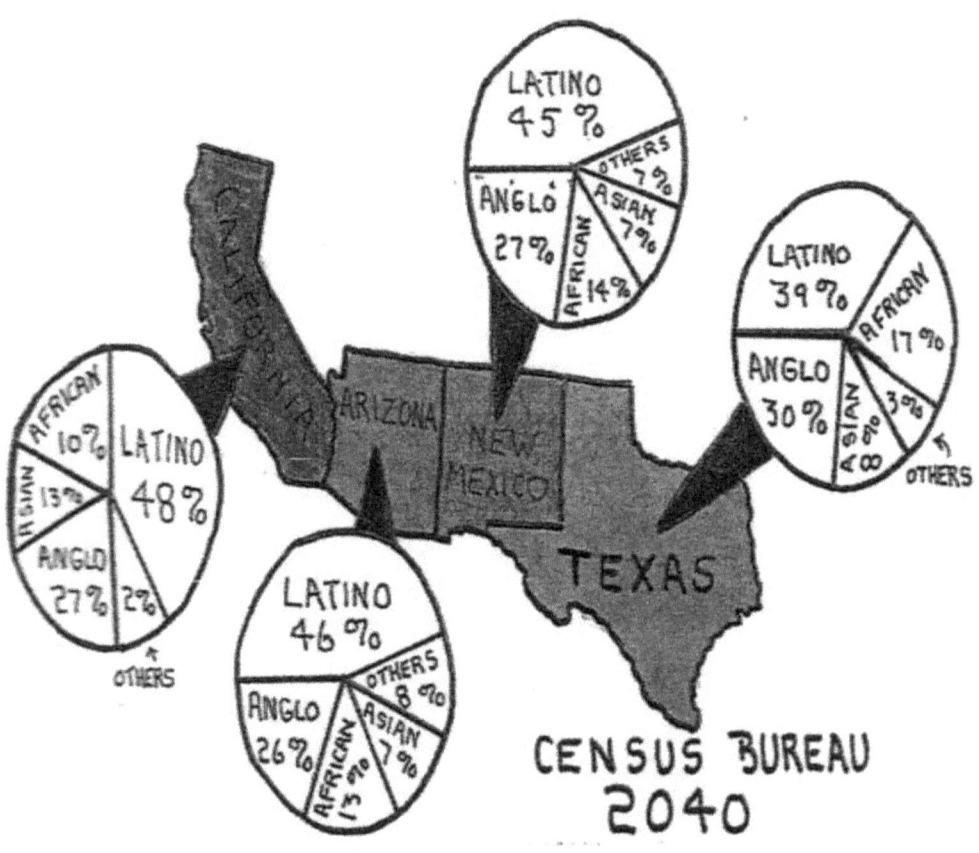

WAVE MEXICANA by Anthony Gordon Pilla

50¢   San Clemente, California   Wednesday, Nov. 3, 2042

LATINO POLITICAL POWER:

LATINO-AMERICANS MAKE UP THE LARGEST ETHNIC GROUP IN THE SOUTHWEST! – CENSUS BUREAU

"A New Political Kid Is On The Block"– Declared Miguel Cairo, Founder and Chairman of L.F.P.: Latino Freedom Party!

He Added, "Within 10 Years the L.F.P. Will Replace the Republican and Democratic Parties As The New Political Power of The Southwest!"

L.F.P.s FIRST TEST OF STRENGTH CAME IN THE "OFF-YEAR" CONGRESSIONAL ELECTION OF '42!

L.F.P. CAPTURED 15 HOUSE SEATS HELD BY DEMOCRATS AND 9 HELD BY REPUBLICANS!

L.F.P. WON: 12 SEATS IN CALIFORNIA, 1 IN ARIZONA, 2 IN NEW MEXICO AND 9 IN TEXAS!

SANTA CRUZ OTTER

65¢   *Santa Cruz, California*   *Wednesday, November 5, 2054*

⋆⋆ELECTION RESULTS - 2054⋆⋆

LATINO FREEDOM PARTY WINS U.S. SENATE SEAT IN CALIFORNIA!

MAYOR JOSE REYES OF SANTA CRUZ UNSEATS REPUBLICAN SENATOR CAROL NIXON!

L.F.P. CANDIDATES TO STATE LEGISLATURE IN 40% OF HOUSE SEATS + 18 SENATE SEATS

L.F.P. CAPTURES 60% OF STATE URBAN ELECTIONS!

L.F.P. REPORTED TO HAVE WON BIG IN: ARIZONA - NEW MEXICO - TEXAS!

WAVE MEXICANA by Anthony Gordon Pilla

LAREDO LONGHORNS
EXTRA EDITION

Vol 86, No. 234   Laredo, Texas   Tuesday, November 5, 2068   65¢

ELECTION HIGHLIGHTS – '68

LATINO FREEDOM PARTY (L.F.P.) WINS MAJORITY SEATS IN BOTH HOUSES OF THE TEXAS STATE LEGISLATURE

L.F.P. WINS A MAJORITY OF CONGRESSIONAL HOUSE SEATS IN CALIFORNIA AND TEXAS!

YUMA, ARIZONA, L.F.P. MAYOR CLAUDIO CHAVEZ Wins Senate Seat Vacated By The Retiring Senator Adam Foote!

> NEW MEXICO'S GOVERNORSHIP WON BY L.F.P.!
>
> Mayor Ricardo Ramos of Las Cruces Became First Governor of Hispanic Heritage Since Governor Bill Richardson in 2006!

Senator Foote (R-AZ) Served 24 Years!

WAVE MEXICANA by Anthony Gordon Pilla | **47**

1776 AMERICA'S TRICENTENNIAL 2076

AMARILLO CACTUS
CITY EDITION

40   Amarillo, Texas   Wednesday, Nov. 3, 2076   Vol. 99 No. 236

L.F.P.
BIG VICTORY IN SOUTHWEST

LATINO FREEDOM PARTY'S NATIONAL CHAIRMAN, SANTIAGO GRECO, HAILED THE "RETURNS" FROM SOUTHWESTERN STATES!

L.F.P. GAINS SEATS IN CONGRESS!

MAKE UP OF THE NEW HOUSE:
170 - REPUBLICANS
165 - DEMOCRATS
100 - L.F.P.

SENATE COMPOSITION:
48 - GOP
36 - DEMOCRATS
16 - LATINO FREEDOM PARTY.

REPUBLICANS RETAIN CONTROL OF THE WHITE HOUSE - JASON HAMILTON WON RE-ELECTION!

LATINO VOTER REGISTRATION 18% HIGHER THAN THE ELECTION OF '72!

48 | WAVE MEXICANA by Anthony Gordon Pilla

EXTRA
SAN ANGELO PINTO

Vol 145, No. 86 — San Angelo, Texas — Wednesday, Nov. 3, 2084 — 50¢

LFP CLEAN-SWEEP OF ALL SOUTHWEST STATES!

LATINO FREEDOM PARTY WINS GOVERNORSHIPS AND STATE LEGISLATURES IN CALIFORNIA, ARIZONA, NEW MEXICO AND TEXAS!

TWO PARTY CONTROL OF CONGRESS: <u>ENDS</u>

'85 - '86 CONGRESS:

SENATE	HOUSE
46 = REPUBLICANS	173 = L.F.P.
38 = DEMOCRATS	158 = REPUBLICANS
16 = L.F.P.	104 = DEMOCRATS
100 = TOTAL	435 = TOTAL

WAVE MEXICANA by Anthony Gordon Pilla | 49

SAN DIEGO SPIRIT

65¢   San Diego, California   Tuesday, January 7, 2085

PUERTO RICO 51ˢᵗ STATE!

LATINO FREEDOM PARTY DRIVING FORCE IN CONGRESS!

L.F.P. NATIONAL CHAIRMAN PEDRO MONTOYA TOLD THE SAN DIEGO SPIRIT, IN AN EXCLUSIVE INTERVIEW:

"INCREASE LATINO POWER IN THE U.S. SENATE IS OUR GOAL"

WAVE MEXICANA by Anthony Gordon Pilla

230 Pesos Mexico City, Mexico Sunday, December 31, 2086

2086 - YEAR IN REVIEW!

JANUARY – MARCH

National Depression Hits Mexico - Massive Layoffs! "Unrest" Begins Among the Working Poor.

APRIL - JUNE

Unemployement Rises to 23.6% of Work Force! Campus Riots Reported at Many Universities.

*JULY - SEPTEMBER *

Violence and Civil Disorder Erupts in Poor Urban Areas of Mexico City!

* OCTOBER - NOVEMBER *

Urban Riots Resulted in Breakdown in Law and Order!

* DECEMBER *

President Jorge Garcia Orders Military to Restore Order!

MILITARY REFUSES ORDER!

WAVE MEXICANA by Anthony Gordon Pilla | 51

EXTRA — **CINCO DE MAYO** — **ENGLISH EDITION**

230 Pesos   Mexico City, Mexico   Monday, January 1, 2087

NEW YEAR'S EVE

PRESIDENTIAL PALACE: Coup D'État!

AT THE STROKE OF MIDNIGHT 2087

MILITARY FORCES, LOYAL TO ARMY CHIEF-OF-STAFF, GENERAL ROBERTO CASTRO ARRESTED PRESIDENT JORGE GARCIA AND SEIZED TOTAL CONTROL OF THE FEDERAL GOVERNMENT IN MEXICO CITY! MOST STATE GOVERNORS DECLARED THEIR LOYALTY TO GENERAL ROBERTO CASTRO!

PRESIDENT JORGE GARCIA WAS CHARGED WITH CORRUPTION AND GROSS VIOLATIONS OF THE MEXICAN FEDERAL CONSTITUTION!

WAVE MEXICANA by Anthony Gordon Pilla

Mexico City, Mexico Monday, January 20, 2087

GENERAL ROBERTO CASTRO DECLARED:

MARTIAL LAW
&
LOYALTY OATH
FROM THE FEDERAL CONGRESS!

STATE-OF-THE-UNION ADDRESS:

General Castro Called Upon The People To Support His "Nueva Visión" For Mexico:

1. Restoration of National Pride.
2. **Open** Border With The United States!
3. Dual Citizenship For Millions Of Latinos Living In America!
4. Call On American Congress To Declare America A "Bi-Lingual" Nation!

230 Pesos   Mexico City, Mexico   Friday, December 15, 2089

★★ PRESIDENT-GENERAL-FOR-LIFE ★★

IN AN ADDRESS BEFORE A JOINT SESSION OF THE MEXICAN CONGRESS, YESTERDAY, GENERAL ROBERTO CASTRO, WHO IS FIRMLY IN CONTROL OF THE FEDERAL GOVERNMENT, DECLARED HIMSELF TO BE PRESIDENT-GENERAL FOR LIFE! HE ALSO ANNOUNCED THAT AS OF JANUARY 1, 2090, HE WILL TAKE THE NAME: **ANTONIO LOPEZ DE SANTA ANA II,** IN MEMORY OF MEXICO'S 19th CENTURY HERO!

IN A THUDEROUS OVATION, THE MEXICAN CONGRESS VOTED UNANIMOUS APPROVAL OF HIS ACTION!

54 | WAVE MEXICANA by Anthony Gordon Pilla

230 Pesos   Mexico City, Mexico   Saturday, January 2, 2090

ANTONIO LOPEZ DE SANTA ANA II

PRESIDENT-GENERAL-FOR-LIFE

WAVE MEXICANA by Anthony Gordon Pilla

Final **DEL RIO SPURS**

Weather: Rain & Cool | Del Rio, Texas | Tuesday, January 29, 2090 | 65¢

LATINOS SWEEP SOUTHWEST

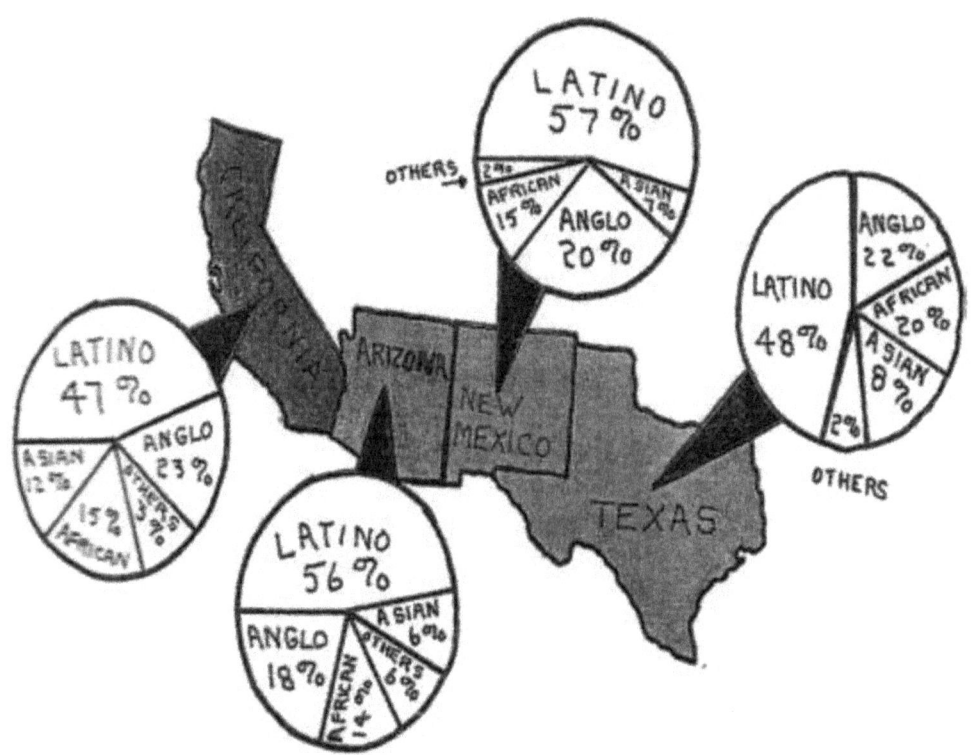

CENSUS BUREAU 2090

WAVE MEXICANA by Anthony Gordon Pilla

# AUSTIN LATINO ★ CITY EDITION

ENGLISH EDITION   **AUSTIN, TEXAS**   **FRIDAY, AUGUST 7, 2090**   **75¢**

O.A.S. - 2090

Speaking before the Organization of American States in Lima, Peru, President-General Santa Ana II predicted a "New Era of Military Rule" was coming to the Americas!

Corrupt civil authority has lost touch with the common man. The trend started 130 years ago with Fidel Castro's New Cuba!

During the decades of 2060's and 2070's we have seen military come to: Peru, Chile, Argentina and Venezuela!

More recently Mexico was added to the rank-of-nations that embraced military over civil authority!

He also stated that military rule is: safe, secure, orderly. Quality of life has grown for the people under effective military leadership.

WAVE MEXICANA by Anthony Gordon Pilla

Final DEL RIO SPURS

Weather: Sunny & Warm | Del Rio, Texas | Wednesday, Nov. 3, 2090

L.F.P. GOVERNOR RAUL SANCHEZ WINS BIG IN TEXAS!

DEFEATS HOUSTON REPUBLICAN MAYOR JON GOLDEN: 54.6% - 45.4%

LATINO FREEDOM PARTY RETAINS CONTROL OF TEXAS STATE LEGISLATURE

House of Representatives
- **L.F.P.** — 113 Seats
- **Democrats** — 76 Seats
- **GOP** — 69 Seats

Senate
- **L.F.P.** — 31 Seats
- **Democrats** — 18 Seats
- **GOP** — 11 Seats

WAVE MEXICANA by Anthony Gordon Pilla

AUSTIN LATINO ★ CITY EDITION

ENGLISH EDITION   AUSTIN, TEXAS   TUESDAY, DECEMBER 7, 2091   75¢

LEGISLATURE TO DEBATE L.F.P BILL TO INVOKE 1845 AUTHORITY TO CREATE 4 NEW STATES!

Annexation of Texas. Joint Resolution of the Congress of the United States, March 1, 1845

New states, of convenient size, not exceeding four in number, in addition to said state of Texas, and having sufficient population, may hereafter, by the consent of said state, be formed out of the territory thereof, which shall be entitled to admission under the provision of the federal constitution.

J.W. JONES
Speaker of the House of Representatives

WILLIE P. MAGNUM
President, pro tempore, of the Senate.

Approv'd March 1, 1845
JOHN TYLER

GOP:

WE REPUBLICANS WILL FIGHT THIS "OUTRAGEOUS" IDEA!

WAVE MEXICANA by Anthony Gordon Pilla

AUSTIN LATINO ★ CITY EDITION

ENGLISH EDITION — AUSTIN, TEXAS — THURSDAY, MARCH 18, 2092 — 75¢

GREAT TEXAS DEBATE

FILIBUSTER BATTLE IN STATE LEGISLATURE OVER 5-STATE BILL! SHARP ATTACKS HEARD ON HOUSE CHAMBER FLOOR!

GOP vs. LFP LEADERS!

L.F.P. MAJORITY LEADER, RICARDO REYES, STATED THAT HISTORY WAS ON THEIR SIDE! THE 1845 RESOLUTION WAS APPROVED BY BOTH U.S. CONGRESS AND THE TEXAS CONGRESS

JOINED BY DEMOCRATIC PARTY LAWMAKERS, L.F.P WAS ABLE TO INVOKE CLOTURE RULE 22-ENDING DEBATE

STRONG OPPOSITION TO 5-STATES BILL BY REPUBLICANS, LEAD BY MINORITY LEADER, TUCKER ADAMS

"WE WILL TIE-UP THIS PLACE FOR MONTHS!"
SAID GOP LEADER ADAM

STATE-WIDE POLLS:
SUPPORT FILIBUSTER - 27%
OPPOSE FILIBUSTER – 73%

DEBATE ENDS!
House OK'd Bill:
164 to 139!

WAVE MEXICANA by Anthony Gordon Pilla

EL PASO LONE STAR

Evening Edition   El Paso, Texas   Friday, March 19, 2092   75¢

ENDING TWO WEEKS OF ANGRY-HEATED DEBATE, THE TEXAS SENATE PASSED, BY TWO VOTES, THE 5 STATES BILL!

L.F.P. MAJORITY, PABLO GOMEZ, HAILED THE VOTE AS "JUSTICE FOR TEXAS LATINOS!"

G.O.P. MINORITY LEADER, OSWALD LEE, DECLARED, "WE WILL GO TO WASHINGTON!"

WAVE MEXICANA by Anthony Gordon Pilla

AMARILLO CACTUS CITY EDITION

60¢ — Amarillo, Texas — Friday, March 19, 2092

5 STATES-FOR-TEXAS

LAW SIGNED BY GOVERNOR RAUL SANCHEZ IN AUSTIN!

LAW CREATES A NINE MEMBER: **TEXAS 5 STATES COMMISSION** TO DRAW BOUNDARIES FOR 4 NEW STATES, AND TO REVISE BOUNDARIES FOR THE STATE OF TEXAS! COMMISSION HAS 18 MONTHS TO CONDUCT STATE-WIDE PUBLIC HEARINGS TO ALLOW FOR CITIZENS' INPUT.

FINAL REPORT MUST BE SUBMITTED TO GOVERNOR SANCHEZ FOR HIS APPROVAL, NO LATER THAN NOVEMBER 1, 2093!

GOP APPEAL LAW TO U.S. SUPREME COURT!

WAVE MEXICANA by Anthony Gordon Pilla

PECOS TUMBLEWEED
NITE EDITION

55¢ | Pecos, Texas | Tuesday, April 11, 2092 | Vol. 146, No. 187

TEXAS REPUBLICAN LEADERS:
TUCKER ADAMS AND OSWALD LEE
PETITIONED THE U.S. SUPREME COURT TO DECLARE THE 5-STATES LAW UNCONSTITUTIONAL!

SUPREME COURT AGREED TO HEAR THE CASE

L.F.P. AND G.O.P.

LAWYERS PRESENTED ARGUMENTS BEFORE THE SUPREME COURT ON DECEMBER 7, 2092.

L.F.P. Position:

Congress, in 1845, passed a Joint-Resolution calling for the Annexation of Texas into the Union. Texas could subdivide into 5 states. Four new states, plus the state of Texas!

G.O.P. Position:

Since Texas was an independent nation in 1845, Congress could only annex Texas by a treaty! A Joint-Resolution does not have the rank of a legal document between nations!

WAVE MEXICANA by Anthony Gordon Pilla | 63

SAN ANTONIO R🌹SE

| 75¢ | San Antonio, Texas | Monday, January 27, 2093 |

TEXAS 5-STATES LAW "CONSTITUTIONAL!"

UNITED STATES SUPREME COURT RULES - 5 to 4:

"A VERY HISTORIC RULING BY THE HIGHEST COURT IN THE LAND, AND ALL LATINO-AMERICANS SHOULD BE PROUD."

A STATEMENT ISSUED BY L.F.P. STATE LEADER, CONSUELO DEL RIO.

GREAT SEAL OF TEXAS

LEGISLATIVE DIGEST

Vol. 129, No.6, October 16, 2093

**TEXAS
FIVE STATES
COMMISSION
FINAL REPORT
★ 2093 ★**

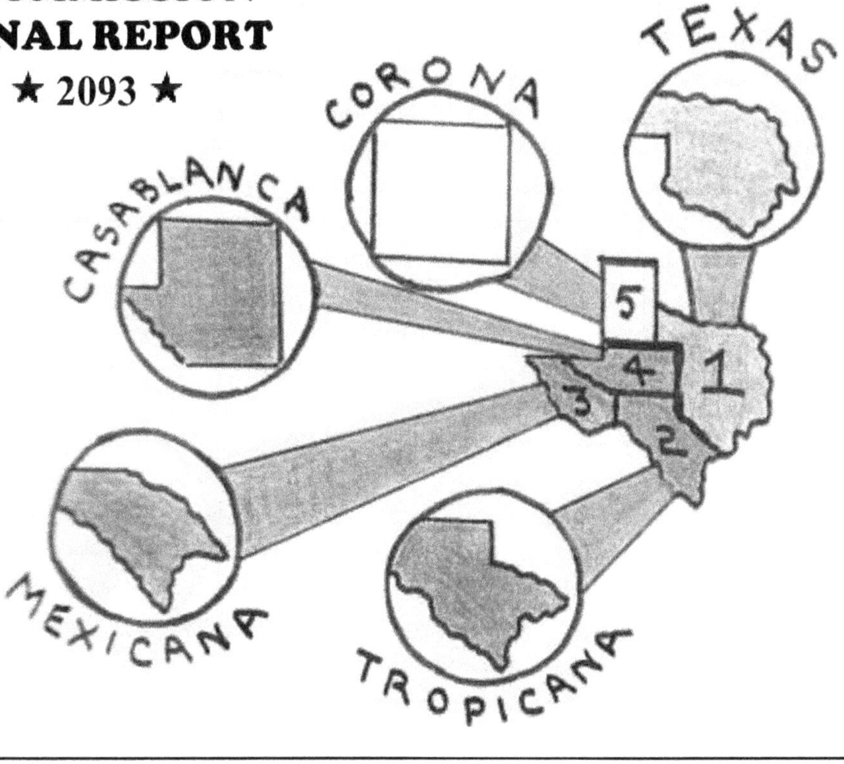

AUSTIN LATINO ★ CITY EDITION

ENGLISH EDITION   **AUSTIN, TEXAS**   **MONDAY, NOVEMBER 22, 2093**   **75¢**

GOVERNOR SANCHEZ SIGNS INTO LAW TEXAS 5-STATES COMMISSION FINAL REPORT

STATE OF TEXAS

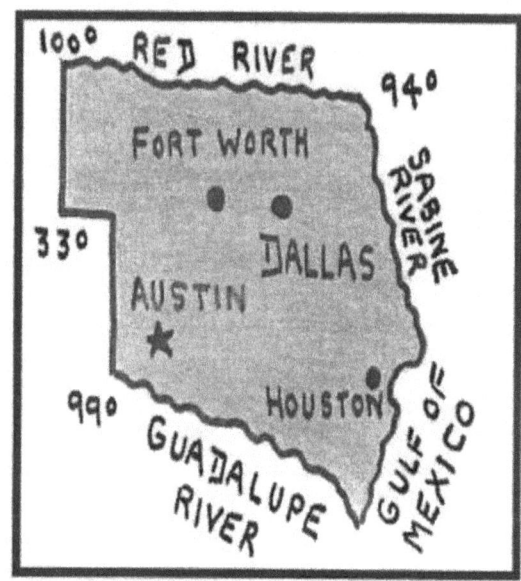

L.F.P. LEGISLATIVE LEADERS: RICARDO REYES AND PABLO GOMEZ STATED, "FULL DEMOCRACY IS NOW FOR ALL LATINO-AMERICANS."

G.O.P. MINORITY LEADERS WERE UNAVAILABLE FOR COMMENTS.

AUSTIN POLL RESULTS:
YES - 33%
NO - 67%

TUCKER ADAMS AND OSWALD LEE WERE REPORTED TO HAVE LEFT AUSTIN!

WAVE MEXICANA by Anthony Gordon Pilla

SAN ANTONIO ROSE

Weather: Rosy   San Antonio, Tropicana   Monday, November 22, 2093   65¢

GOVERNOR RAUL SANCHEZ MADE IT OFFICIAL:

TEXAS IS NOW FIVE STATES

SAN ANTONIO IS NOW THE CAPITAL OF OUR STATE: **TROPICANA**

L.F.P.

LED FIGHT FOR STATEHOOD AND WON!

REPUBLICANS

STRONGLY OPPOSED THE "BREAK-UP" OF TEXAS! TOOK THEIR FIGHT TO D.C. AND LOST!

POLL:
YES: 68% | NO: 32%

WAVE MEXICANA by Anthony Gordon Pilla

PEC🌵S TUMBLEWEED
NITE EDITION

| 55¢ | Pecos, Mexicana | Monday, November 22, 2093 | Vol. 147, No. 16 |

GOVERNOR RAUL SANCHEZ
GIVES HIS **O.K.** TO **TEXAS 5 STATES COMMISSION'S** FINAL REPORT!

EL PASO IS NOW THE CAPITAL OF OUR NEW STATE OF MEXICANA.

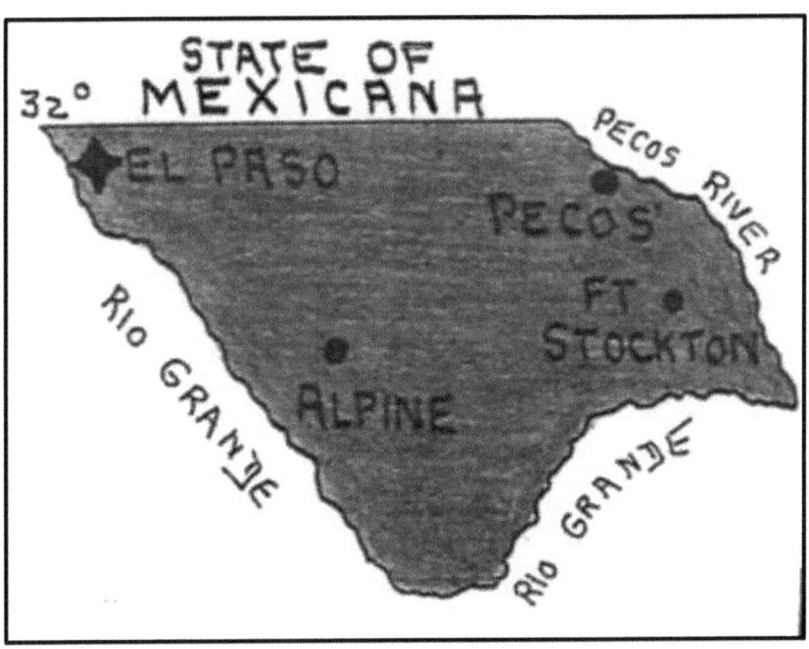

TEXAS REPUBLICAN LEADERS, AFTER LOSING ISSUE IN AUSTIN POLL TOOK THE CONFLICT TO THE U.S. SUPREME COURT. BY A VOTE OF 5 To 4, THE COURT REJECTED THEIR ARGUMENTS!

P.T. POLL RESULTS:

73% APPROVED

27% DISAPPROVED

WAVE MEXICANA by Anthony Gordon Pilla

EXTRA
SAN ANGELO PINTO

Vol 157, No. 109   San Angelo, Casablanca   Monday, November 22, 2093   20¢

IT'S OFFICIAL:

AUSTIN OK'S 5-STATE PLAN!

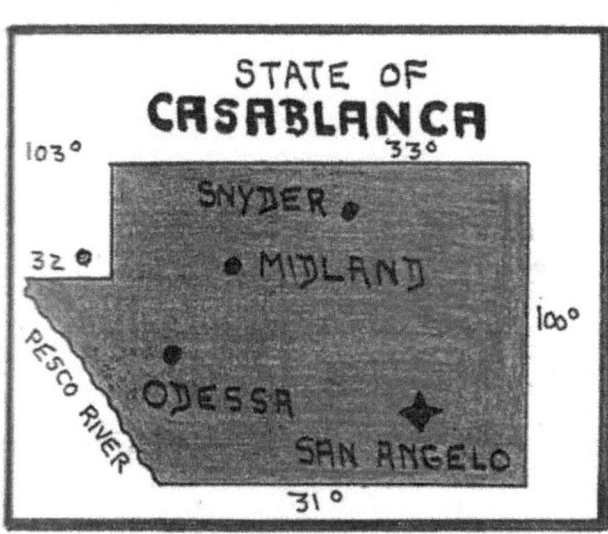

POLL RESULTS:
YES - 71%
NO - 23%
??? - 6%

We will now be called:
CITIZENS OF CASABLANCA

SAN ANGELO is our state capital!

"GREAT DAY FOR ALL LATINOS"
Declared National Leader of the LATINO FREEDOM PARTY: Luis Polo

REPUBLICANS APPEALED ISSUE TO THE SUPREME COURT AND LOST THEIR FIGHT 5 TO 4!

WAVE MEXICANA by Anthony Gordon Pilla | 69

AMARILLO CACTUS CITY EDITION

60¢ | Amarillo, Corona | Monday, Novemeber 22, 2093 | Vol. 1, No. 1

GOODBYE PAN HANDLE
HELLO CORONA!

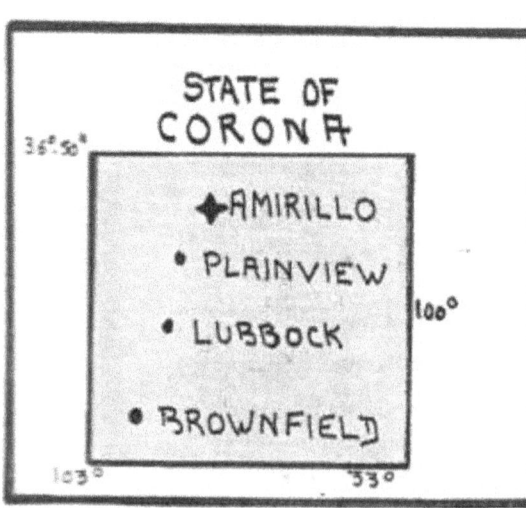

AUSTIN GRANTS US STATEHOOD

AMARILLO BECOMES STATE CAPITAL

Latino Freedom party won a big victory in Austin and Washington!

G.O.P. LEADERS WENT TO WASHINGTON, D.C., HOPING TO CONVINCE THE SUPREME COURT TO SIDE WITH THEM
THEY LOST THEIR FIGHT!

"TAILGATE" PARTIES REPORTED ALL OVER CORONA!!!

WAVE MEXICANA by Anthony Gordon Pilla

SAN ANTONIO ROSE

Weather: Rain　　San Antonio, Tropicana　　Tuesday, January 10, 2094　　65¢

ESTABLISHING CLOSER RELATIONS:
MEXICO AND NEW BORDER STATES...

MEXICANA AND TROPICANA!

- ❖ CINCO DE MAYO DECLARED A "STATE HOLIDAY".
- ❖ "BI-LINGUAL" CLASSES IN ALL PUBLIC SCHOOLS!
- ❖ STUDY OF MEXICAN HISTORY REQUIRED FOR ALL STUDENTS.
- ❖ "WELCOME WAGONS" LOCATED AT ALL BORDER CROSSINGS.
- ❖ ALL PUBLIC SIGNS ARE TO BE IN SPANISH AND ENGLISH.
- ❖ BI-LINGUAL PROCEEDINGS IN ALL STATE AND LOCAL COURTS, POLICE DEPARTMENTS, PUBLIC HEARINGS AND EVENTS!

YUMA DESERT SUN

WEATHER: HOT

Vol. 128, No. 79 — Yuma, Arizona — Monday, July 16, 2094 — 75¢

LATINO-BLACK CAUCUS CONNECTION

REP. ANGEL FERRER (LFP-AZ) AND SENATOR JESSIE ARMSTRONG (D-NY) HAVE UNITED ON ISSUES BOTH CAUCUS WANT CONGRESS TO VOTE FOR!

THEIR COMBINED FORCES SHOULD ACHIEVE "VETO PROOF" PASSAGE:

PRIORITY ITEMS:

1. DECLARE AMERICA A "BI-LINGUAL" NATION! SPANISH AND ENGLISH - OFFICIAL LANGUAGES FOR ALL PUBLIC MATTERS. PUBLIC SCHOOLS ARE RFQUIRED TO TEACH BOTH LANGUAGES TO ALL STUDENTS.
2. DUAL-CITIZEN SHIP FOR ALL LATINO AMERICANS!
3. "OPEN BORDERS" WITH MEXICO!
4. STATEHOOD FOR THE DISTRICT OF COLUMBIA!

SAN DIEGO SPIRIT

75¢   San Diego, California   Monday, November 11, 2109

STATEHOOD FOR SHASTA

SACRAMENTO AND WASHINGTON APPROVED SHASTA JOINING THE UNION AS THE 56th STATE!

L.F.P. LEADERS, IN A SURPRISE MOVE. SUPPORTED REPUBLICAN EFFORTS TO CREATE NEW STATE OF SHASTA.

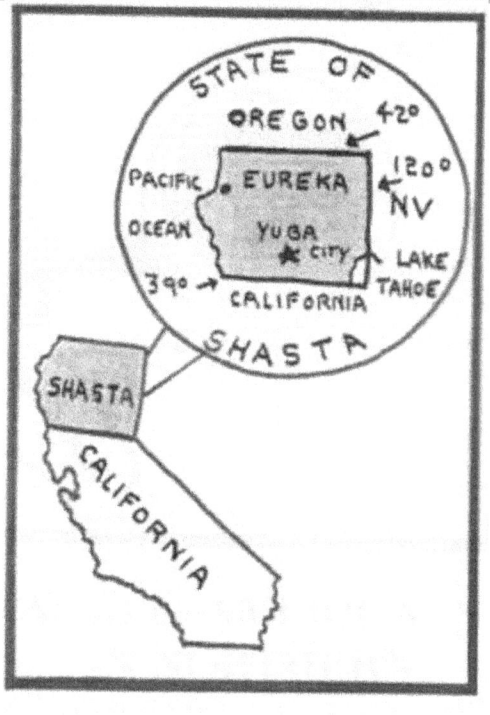

ANGLO-AMERICAN'S IN NORTHERN CALIFORNIA, LED BY REPUBLICAN STATE CAPITAL LEADER WILLIAM GRANT, WON THE RIGHT TO SECEDE WILL BE FROM THE STATE OF CALIFORNIA!

State Capital for Shasta will be

YUBA CITY!

SANTA CRUZ OTTER

85¢   *Santa Cruz, California*   *Tuesday, November 12, 2109*

ATLANTIC AND PACIFIC "A+P" STATEHOOD COMPROMISE!

CONGRESS, IN A RARE UNITY MOOD, VOTED TO ADMIT <u>SHASTA</u> AND <u>COLUMBIA</u> AS THE 56th AND 57th STATES TO THE UNION!

STATEHOOD BEGINS: JANUARY 1st, 2110!

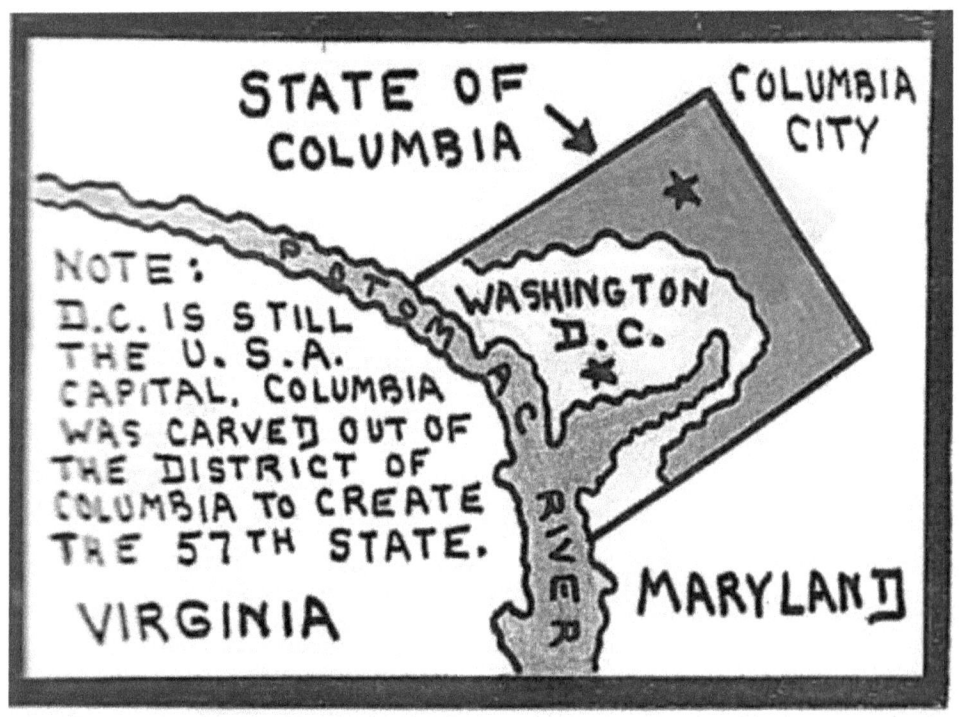

WAVE MEXICANA by Anthony Gordon Pilla

SAN ANTONIO ROSE

Weather: Cold   San Antonio, Tropicana   Thursday, November 30, 2109   85¢

IN A SHOW OF SOLIDARITY WITH MEXICO, THE NATION'S LARGEST POLITICAL PARTY **(L.F.P.)** LATINO FREEDOM PARTY- **UNVEILED ITS PARTY'S FLAG** AT L.F.P. NATIONAL HEADQUARTERS IN WASHINGTON D.C.

WAVE MEXICANA by Anthony Gordon Pilla

EL PASO LONE ST★R

Evening Edition El Paso, Mexicana Monday, December 17, 2115 85¢

TREACHERY ON A GRAND SCALE:

MEXICO PLOTS WITH L.F.P TO TAKE BACK SOUTHWESTERN STATES!

SANTA ANA II VISION: PAN MEXICANA!

Latino Freedom Party leaders held in secret talks with President-General Santa Ana II and Junta military leaders.

Operation: "Pan-Mexicana" was developed

Map of 1820 Adams – Onis Treaty

EXCLUSIVE TO THE LONESTAR: AT A RECENT EL PASO MEETING, CARLOS ROSA, NATIONAL CHAIRMAN OF THE L.F.P. ENDORSED THE PAN-AMERICA PLOT AND URGED L.F.P REGIONAL LEADERS TO JOIN HIS ENDORSEMENT!

75¢   San Clemente, California   Tuesday, December 18, 2115

PAN MEXICANA PLOT

AT A MOUNTAIN RESORT IN DURANGO, MEXICO. LAST OCTOBER, A SECRET MEETING WAS HELD BETWEEN MEXICAN OFFICIALS AND LEADERS OF THE LATINO FREEDOM PARTY!

PRESIDENT SANTA ANA II STATED THAT PAN-MEXICANA WAS HIS GOAL FOR MILLIONS OF LATINOS ON "BOTH SIDES OF THE BORDER."

"WITH HELP FROM THE L.F.P., WE WILL RESTORE OUR BORDERS WITH THE UNITED STATES BASED ON THE 1820 ADAMS-ONIS TREATY." THIS WOULD RETURN TO MEXICO: AMERICA'S SOUTHWEST!

SANTA ANA RECALLED A LATINO YOUTH'S 2005 BATTLE CRY:

"THIS LAND WAS ONCE MEXICAN AND INDIAN TERRITORY – **SOME DAY BACK TO MEXICO!**"

SANTA FE TRAIL

Vol. 146, No. 12   Santa Fe, New Mexico   Monday, January 10, 2116   85¢

ROSA-SANTA ANA CONNECTION

"RANK AND FILE" OUTRAGED L.F.P. MEMBERS STRONGLY PROTESTED WHAT THEIR PARTY CHIEF, CARLOS ROSA, DID BEHIND THEIR BACKS!

FIRESTORM OF ANGER AND SHOCK SPREAD LIKE WILDFIRE THROUGHOUT THE SOUTHWESTERN STATES!

THOUSANDS OF LOYAL LATINO-AMERICANS: L.F.P., REPUBLICANS AND DEMOCRATS, ALL OVER AMERICA, CALLED UPON PRESIDENT NELSON EDDIE TO BREAK DIPLOMATIC RELATIONS WITH THE SANTA ANA'S MILITARY GOVERNMENT!

SEAL OUR BORDER - USE THE ARMY!

250 Pesos   Mexico City, Mexico   Saturday, March 3, 2117

MILLIONS OF PEOPLE TAKE TO THE STREETS! YOUNG MILITARY OFFICERS "BREAK" WITH SANTA ANA II AND LAUNCH THE

2117 CACTUS REVOLT!

STANDING BEHIND THEIR 2117 FLAG,

THEY TOOK CONTROL OF GOV'T HOUSE,

AND LAY SIEGE TO THE PALACE
– ISOLATING SANTA ANA!

VATICAN CITY GIVES MORAL AND SPIRITUAL SUPPORT TO THE CACTUS REVOLT!
POPE ADOLPH LEO I CALLED ON SANTA ANA II, PRESIDENT OF MEXICO, TO RESIGN! ENDING 30 YEARS OF MILITARY RULE!

WAVE MEXICANA by Anthony Gordon Pilla

250 Pesos　　　　　Mexico City, Mexico　　　　　Sunday, March 4, 2117

MAJOR PEDRO CUGAT
DEPUTY COMMANDER MEXICO CITY MILITARY DISTRICT

VITA

AGE: 35
BORN: 2082, Tampico
EDUCATION: Catholic Schools
GRADUATED: 2100
  (Rank -12 out of 165)
COLLEGE: Mexico War College
- 2100-2104
- Commissioned: 2nd
- Ranked 7th out of 286

YUCATAN Military District:
- '04 – '09
- Commissioned: 1st Lt. & Captain

MEXICO CITY Military District
- 21 10-21 17 Recruitment and Training Leader
- Personnel Director ('15 – 'S17)
- Commissioned: Major

RESIGNED COMMISSION:
January 1, 2117

LEADER: Cactus Revolt Army

80 | WAVE MEXICANA by Anthony Gordon Pilla

250 Pesos · Mexico City, Mexico · Friday, March 10, 2117

LAST HOURS OF
SANTA ANA II
AS PRESIDENT-GENERAL:
March 9, 2117!

1:15 AM: SANTA ANA (ROBERTO CASTRO) TELEPHONES HIS COUSIN IN HAVANA - CUBA'S PRESIDENT TINO – CASTRO - EOR EXILE STATUS 1N HAVANA! TINO IMMEDIATELY ORDERS A MILITARY JET TO PICK UP SANTA ANA IN MEXICO CITY!

4:30 AM: ROBERTO CASTRO AND STAFF BOARD JET UNDER PROTECTION OF LOYAL TROOPS.

5:10 AM: ROBERTO CASTRO SAFELY DEPARTS MEXICO FOR EXILE IN HAVANA, CUBA.

7:45 AM: SANTA ANA GREETED BY HUNDREDS OF TINO CASTRO S LOYALISTS. PRESIDENT CASTRO DECLARES THAT PRESIDENT-GENERAL SANTA ANA II TO BE KNOWN AS

HERO-GENERAL-IN-EXILE

EXTRA — **ENGLISH EDITION**

CINCO DE MAYO

250 Pesos   Mexico City, Mexico   Monday, August 2, 2117

DEMOCRACY RESTORED TO MEXICO!

CACTUS REVOLT LEADERS CONTROL GOVERNMENT

HIGHLIGHTS OF EVENTS

1. Political parties invited to assemble at Government House on July 15, 2115, to elect temporary officers to administer affairs.
2. Congress sets February 2, 2118 as Presidential and Congressional Election Day!
3. Political campaigns to run from September 1, 2117, through January 31, 2118.
4. Congress created a Federal Election Comission to conduct national elections.
5. Congress restores the 2048 Constitution: Law-of-the-Land!

270Pesos   Mexico City, Mexico   Wednesday, August 4, 2117

DEEP THROAT
"PALACE WHISPERS"

CINCO DE MAYO'S ACE REPORTERS: VICENTE GARCIA AND JUAN PADILLA REVEAL IN TODAY'S EDITION - A 30 YEAR OLD SECRET!

WHO WAS DEEP THROAT?

DEEP THROAT - CESAR CORDERO SERVED AS THE No. 2 AGENT IN SANTA ANA II'S PALACE GUARDS! HE GAVE VALUABLE "PALACE WHISPERS," FROM 2087 TO 2117, TO GARCIA AND PADILLA!

* FOLLOW THE MONEY *

1. PRO-SANTA ANA L.F.P. LEADERS: GIVEN LARGE CASH $UMS!

2. HUGE $UMS TO CHURCH OFFICIALS: ENCOURAGE LARGE FAMILIES!

LAREDO LONGHORNS
EXTRA EDITION

Vol 135, No. 222 Laredo, Tropicana Saturday, August 7, 2117 90¢

LONGHORN'S I-TEAM EXCLUSIVE!

I-TEAM CHIEF, FERNANDO POSADA, reports that Mexico's "DEEP THROAT" – Cesar Cordero - gave $150,000 to each L.F.P. delegate who attended the Durango secret meeting in October 2114!

In return they pledged to "push" L.F.P. leaders to publicly *ENDORSE* Santa Ana's **PAN-MEXICANA** scheme!

Chief Posada reveals that church officials received, in cash, millions of dollars to "urge" Mexican families to: "Do-God's-Work" and have large families! A Population Explosion was part of Santa Ana's plan to "over-run" America's southwest with I.A.!

Goal was to have the southwestern states **secede** from America and join Mexico as part of Pan-Mexicana!

275 Pesos — Mexico City, Mexico — Saturday, March 3, 2118

ELECTION RESULTS:

IT'S GONZALEZ IN A LANDSLIDE!

SENATOR ALBERTO GONZALEZ, LIBERTY PARTY'S PRESIDENTIAL CANDIDATE, DEFEATED CONSERVATIVE PARTY CANDIDATE RAMON RODRIGUEZ, MAYOR OF TAMPICO - 56% TO 44%! VOTER TURNOUT WAS THE LARGEST IN ANY MEXICAN ELECTION: 63.7%

LIBERTY PARTY WON CONTROL OF CONGRESS:

185 SEATS TO CONSERVATIVE'S 129 IN THE HOUSE OF DELEGATES! MAKE-UP OF SENATE: 63 (LP) TO 37 (CP)!

INAUGURATION DAY: MARCH 18, '18

EXTRA **CINCO DE MAYO** **ENGLISH EDITION**

275 Pesos   Mexico City, Mexico   Satirday, March 19, 2118

INAUGURATION DAY

ALBERTO GONZALEZ
TAKE OATH OF OFFICE
NOON, MARCH 18, 2118
AT GOVERNMENT HOUSE IN MEXICO CITY

HIGHLIGHTS OF ADDRESS:

1. Santa Ana's Pan-Mexicana scheme declared dead!
2. President promised to restore liberty and freedom!
3. Seek financial help from the United States.
4. Resume travel-trade-commerce With U.S.A.
5. Ordered Foreign Affairs Minister, Carla Lopez, to restore "normal ties" with Washington, D.C.
6. Seek a solution to the century old

BATTLE OF THE BORDERS!

SANTA CRUZ OTTER

95¢ — Santa Cruz, California — Friday, April 4, 2118

WASHINGTON EXTENDS "OLIVE BRANCH" TO MEXICO!

AMERICAN PRESIDENT NELSON EDDIE "VERY PLEASED" WITH ALBERTO GONZALEZ INAUGURAL ADDRESS.

PRESIDENT EDDIE ORDERED:

1. RE-OPEN AMERICAN EMBASSY IN MEXICO CITY
2. EXCHANGE AMBASSADORS
3. REMOVE ALL TRAVEL AND TRADE RESTRICTIONS.
4. ASK CONGRESS FOR 875 BILLION DOLLARS TO HELP RESTORE MEXICO'S ECONOMY.
   GOAL: "ENCOURAGE" MEXICANS **NOT** TO **LEAVE** THEIR COUNTRY - ILLEGALLY!
5. APPOINT VICE PRESIDENT STELLA DALLES TO HEAD A DIPLOMATIC TEAM TO MEET WITH MEXICAN DIPLOMATS.
   MISSION: FIND A **SOLUTION** TO OUR BORDER DISPUTES!

LAREDO LONGHORNS
EXTRA EDITION

Vol 136, No. 191   Laredo, Tropicana   Saturday, September 9, 2118   90¢

INTENSIVE BORDER DIPLOMACY...
BETWEEN MEXICO AND THE UNITED STATES!

DURING THE MONTHS OF JULY AND AUGUST, DIPLOMATS AND MILITARY ADVISORS HELD A SERIES OF MEETINGS, ALTERNATING BETWEEN MEXICALI AND YUMA IN JULY, AND LAREDO AND NUEVO LAREDO IN AUGUST.

ISSUES TO BE RESOLVED:

1. SAFE BORDER CROSSING FOR LEGAL ALIENS.
2. METHODS TO DISCOURAGE I.A. CROSSING.
3. HUMANE AND CIVIL RIGHTS FOR BORDER VIOLATORS.
4. REMOVAL OF WALLS AND BORDER FENCES.
5. WITHDRAW AMERICAN TROOPS FROM THE BORDER.
6. U.S. AND MEXICAN BORDER PATROL TEAMS.

EL PASO LONE STAR

Special Edition   El Paso, Mexicana   Tuesday, September 11, 2118   90¢

128 YEARS OF BORDER BATTLES END ON JANUARY 1, 2119!

The Rio Grande Treaty of 2118 was signed by Mexico's President Albert Gonzalez and America's President Nelson Eddie on a river boat in the middle of the Rio Grand. Today – begins a new era in U.S.A. – Mexican relations Sept. 11, 2118

TREATY CALLS FOR MUTUAL RESPECT, INTEGRITY AND SECURITY FOR BOTH BORDERS. BORDER PATROL TEAMS COMPOSED OF EQUAL NUMBERS OF MEXICAN AND AMERICAN OFFICERS AND INSPECTORS, WILL SEE THAT BOTH BORDERS ARE SECURED AT ALL TIMES!

TREATY IN EFFECT:

JANUARY 1, 2119

275 Pesos   Mexico City, Mexico   Saturday, September 12, 2118

RIO GRANDE TREATY ENDS 128 YEARS OF "BORDER DISPUTE" BETWEEN MEXICO AND THE UNITED STATES

PRESIDENT ALBERTO GONZALEZ OF MEXICO AND PRESIDENT NELSON EDDIE OF THE UNITED STATES SIGNED THE TREATY ON A RIO GRANDE RIVER BOAT NORTH OF CIUDAD JUAREZ AND SOUTH OF EL PASO

TREATY BEGINS JAN. 1, 2119

WAVE MEXICANA by Anthony Gordon Pilla

SAN DIEGO SPIRIT

85¢   San Diego, California   Saturday, January 5, 2119

ALL QUIET...

ON OUR SECURED SOUTHERN BORDER WITH MEXICO

THANKS TO CAPTAINS

JOSE AMADO & TROY HUNTER

JOINT COMMANDERS

BI-NATIONAL BORDER TEAMS

WAVE MEXICANA by Anthony Gordon Pilla

YUMA DESERT SUN

WEATHER: HOT

Vol. 143, No. 20   Yuma, Arizona   Friday, January 20, 2119   85¢

SECURED BORDERS

DAWN OF A NEW ERA BETWEEN:

UNITED STATES AND MEXICO

WAVE MEXICANA by Anthony Gordon Pilla

www.ingramcontent.com/pod-product-compliance
Lightning Source LLC
LaVergne TN
LVHW050025080526
838202LV00069B/6912